Christmas Whimsy

A **WORDPLAY** COLORING BOOK

Jessica Mazurkiewicz

Dover Publications, Inc.
Mineola, New York

Thirty-one whimsical illustrations—brimming with words that bring the spirit of Christmas to mind—make up this delightful holiday coloring book intended for advanced colorists and word enthusiasts. Images and descriptive terms combine to form a Christmas stocking, candy cane, drum, mug of hot chocolate, nutcracker, pair of mittens, ornaments, and many more festive designs. The pages are perforated for easy removal from the book; after coloring these Yuletide drawings, it will be easy to display your WordPlay artwork. It's beginning to look a lot like Christmas!

Bibliographical Note

Christmas Whimsy: A WordPlay Coloring Book is a new work, first published by Dover Publications, Inc., in 2017.

International Standard Book Number

ISBN-13: 978-0-486-81375-2
ISBN-10: 0-486-81375-4

Manufactured in the United States by LSC Communications
81375402   2017
www.doverpublications.com

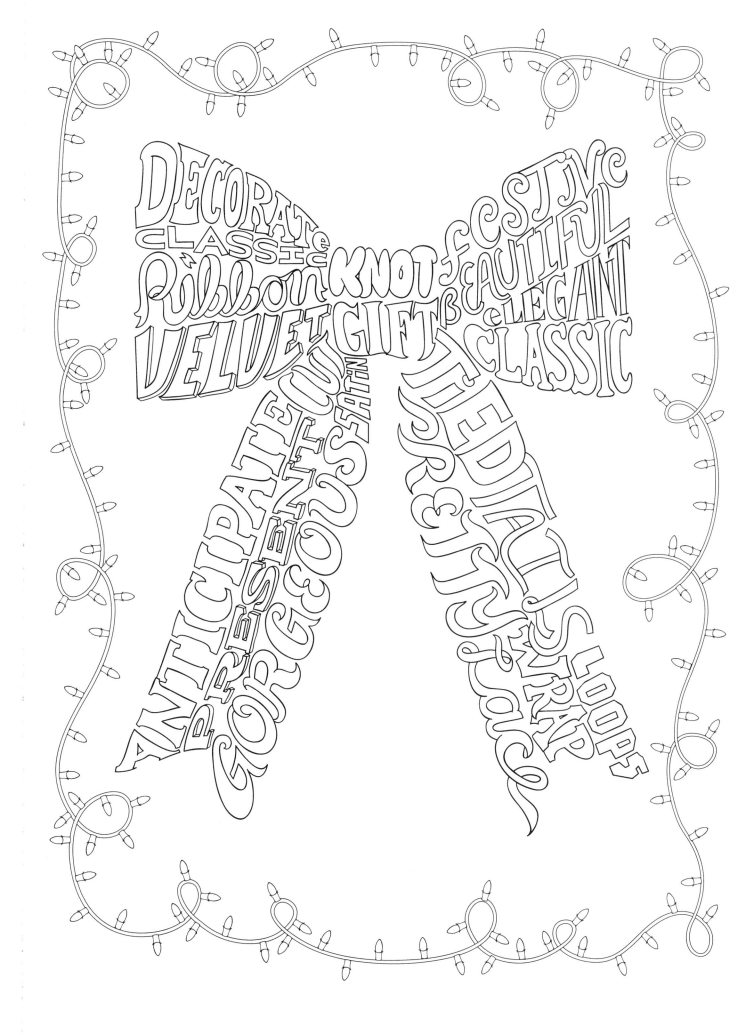

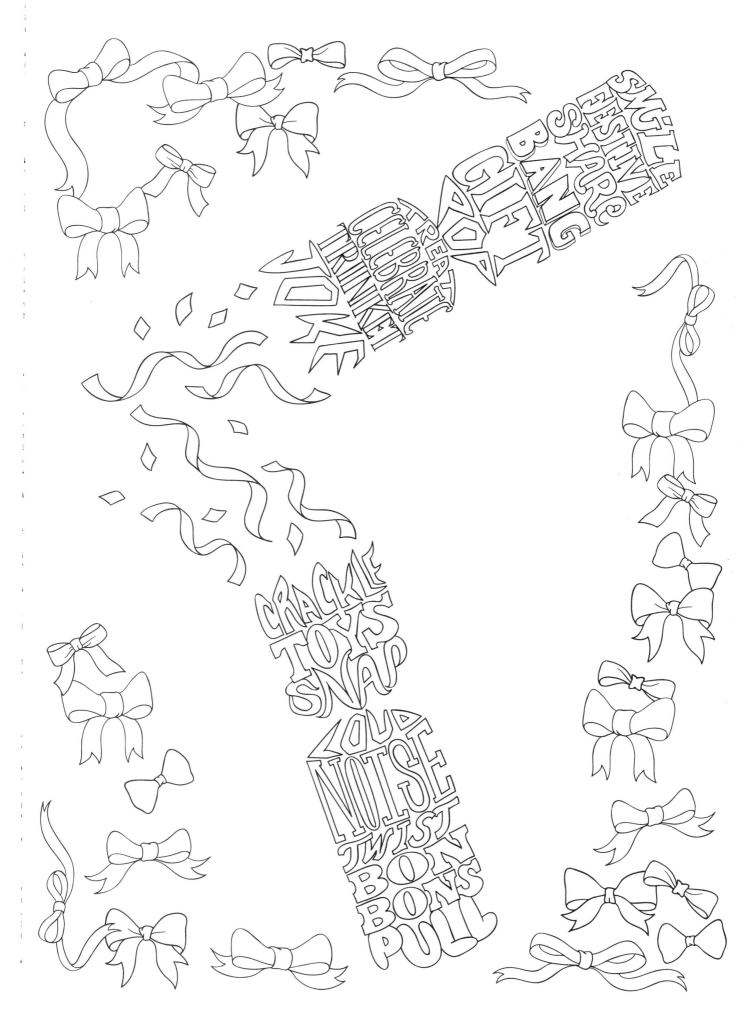

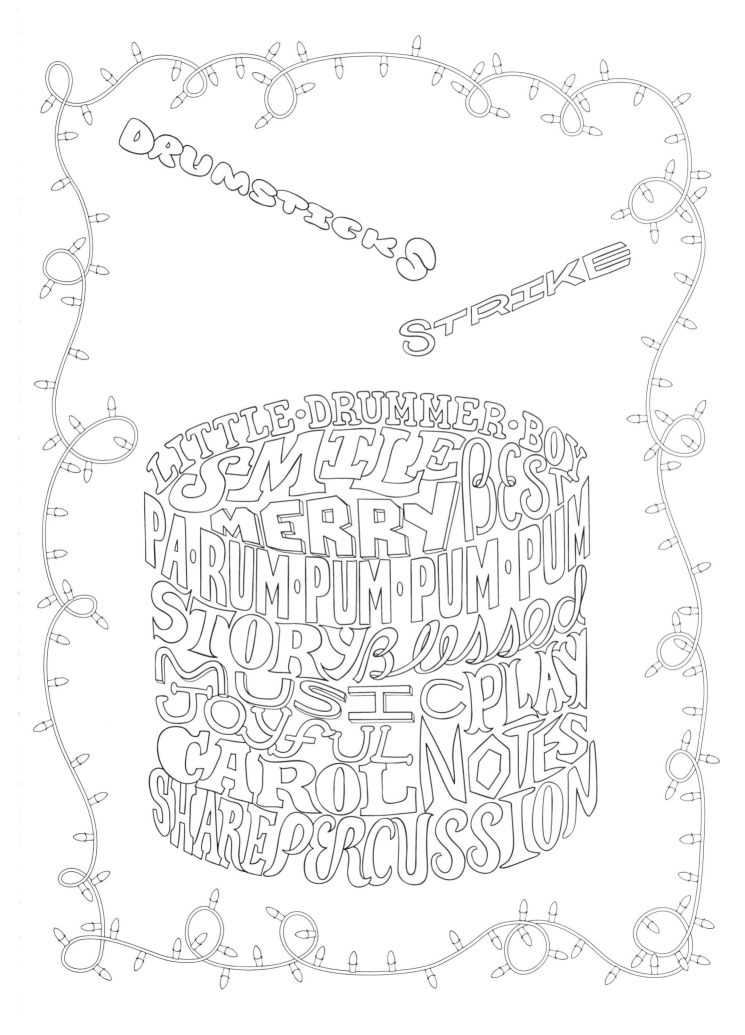